The Moon, the Sun and All the Constellations Beginner's Astronomy Lessons for Kids

Children's Astronomy & Space Books

pfiffikus

EDUCATIONAL BOOKS FOR CHILDREN K-12

Do you ever wonder what those twinkling things or that big shining circle in the night sky are? What about that blazing object in the morning sky? Read on and learn more about them.

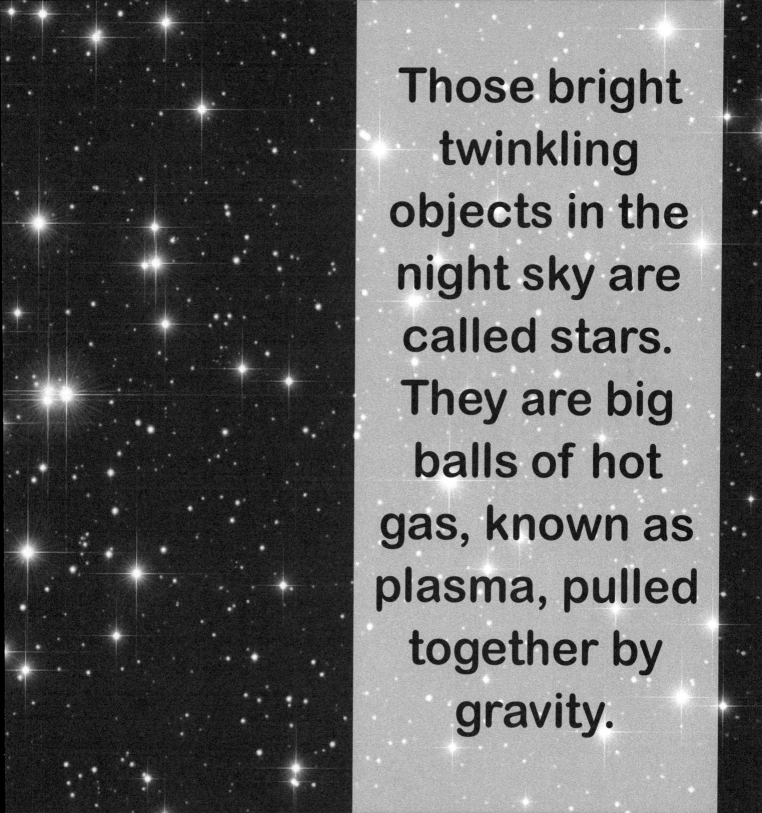

Those bright twinkling objects in the night sky are called stars. They are big balls of hot gas, known as plasma, pulled together by gravity.

Most stars are aged between 1 to 100 billion years old.

The hottest star
is blue while
the coolest
star is red.

Stars may look like they twinkle but they do not! They only look like it because of the sudden movement in the earth's atmosphere.

When stars form a pattern in the night sky, it is called a star constellation.

Constellations can take many forms, like a shape of an animal, man, woman, and/or any other objects.

Constellation comes from the Latin term, "cōnstellātiō", which means a set of stars.

There are
88 official
constellations,
48 of which
are ancient
constellations
discovered
by Greek
astronomer
Ptolemy.

We cannot see all 88 constellations since some are visible only in the northern hemisphere while others are only visible in the southern hemisphere.

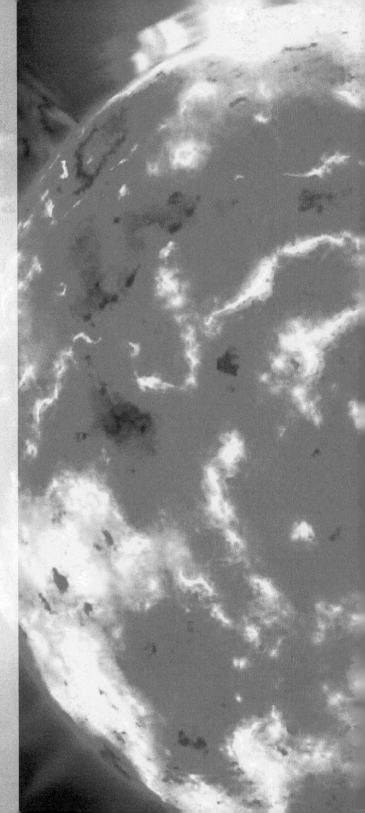

The Sun is the bright yellow sphere we see every morning. All planets orbit around it.

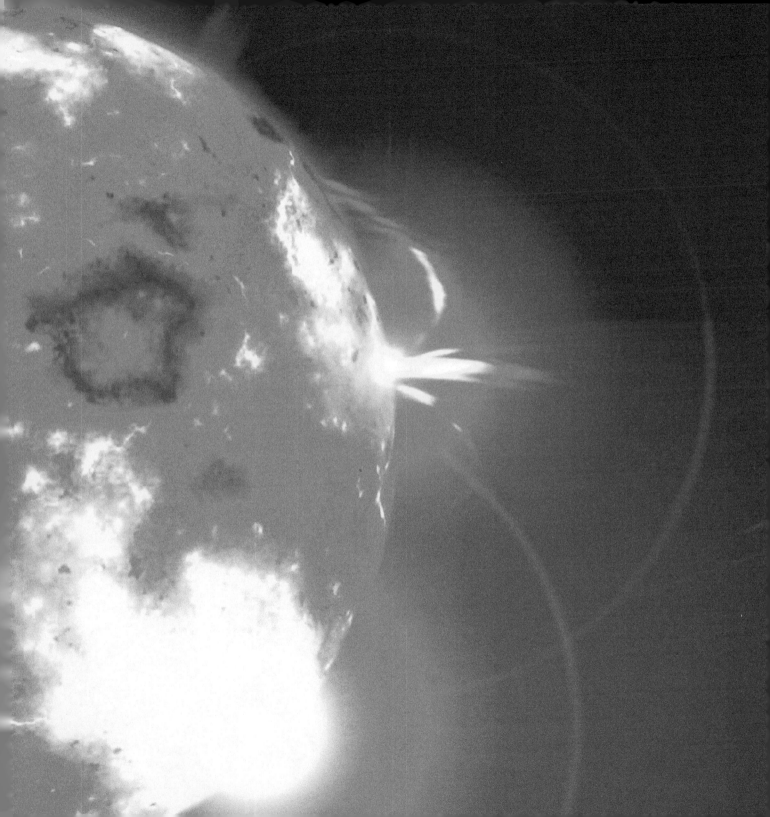

The Sun is also a star, but it is the only known star that does not belong to any constellation.

It is so big
that one
million Earths
could fit in it!

The Sun is very hot. Its temperature could reach 15 million degree Celsius!

The bright yellow sphere we see at night is the Moon.

Contrary to the Sun, it is the moon that orbits our planet. It is the only natural satellite of the Earth.

The first person to land on the Moon was Neil Armstrong.

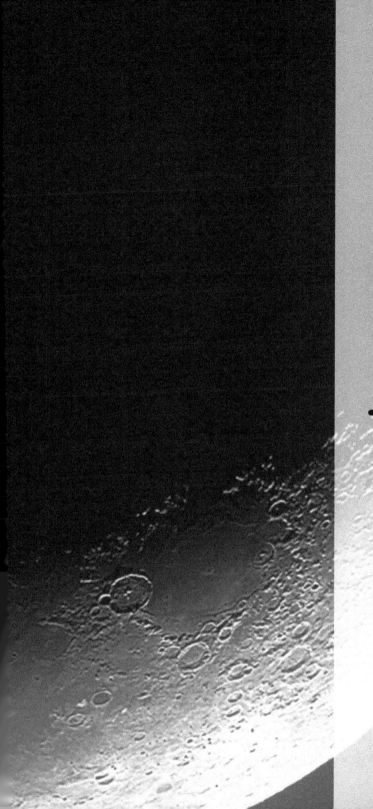

The Moon also has mountains. The largest is called Mons Huygens.

There is much more to know about the Sun, Stars and Moon. Research and have fun!